This Coloring Book
Belongs to:

_____

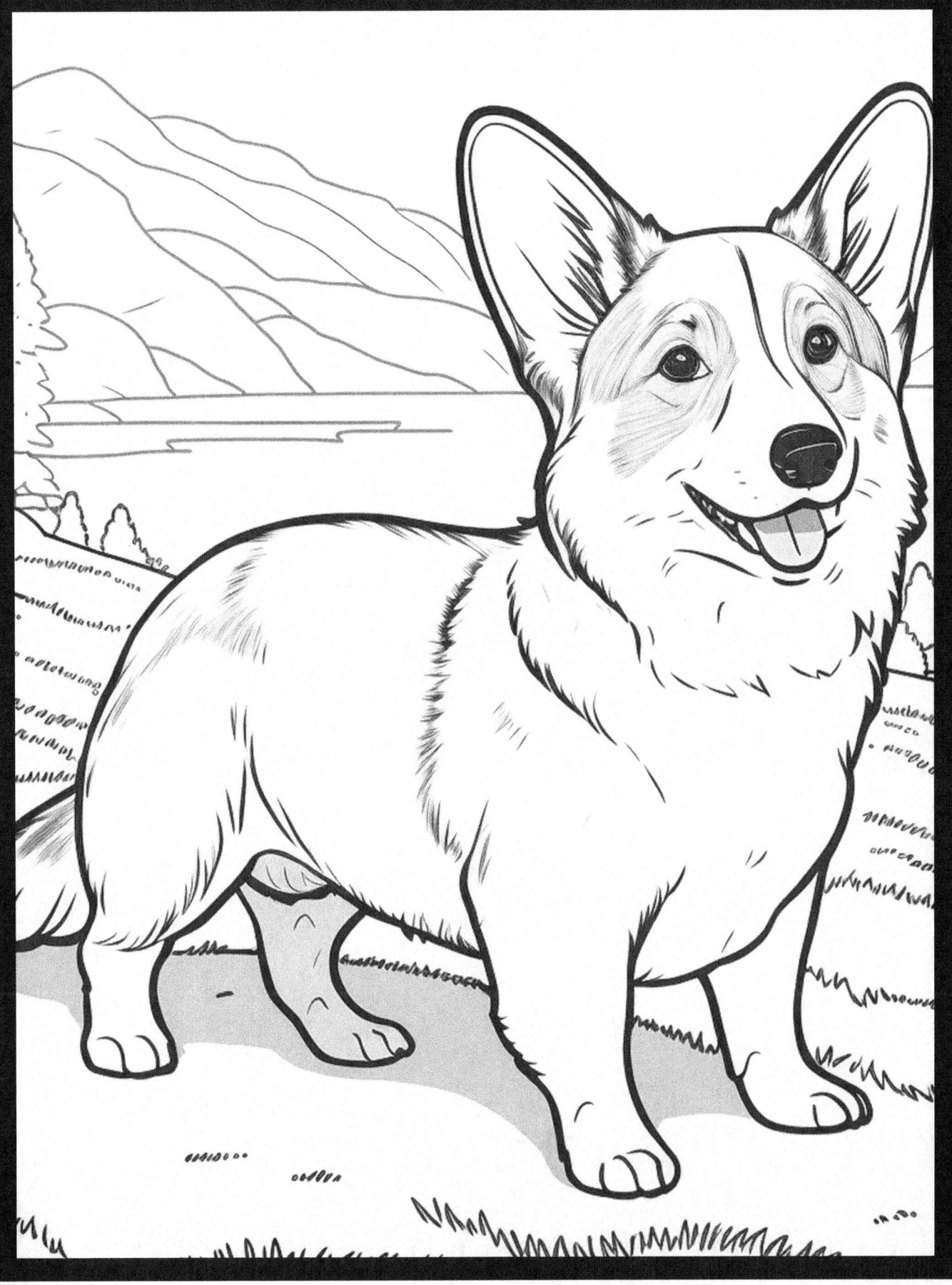

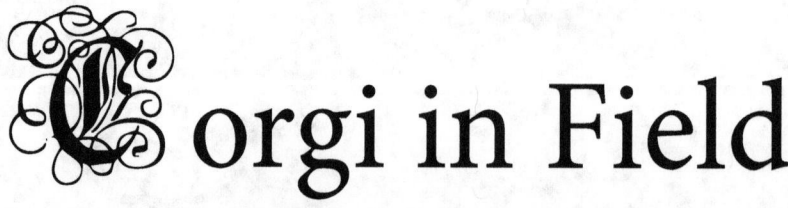

Corgi in Field

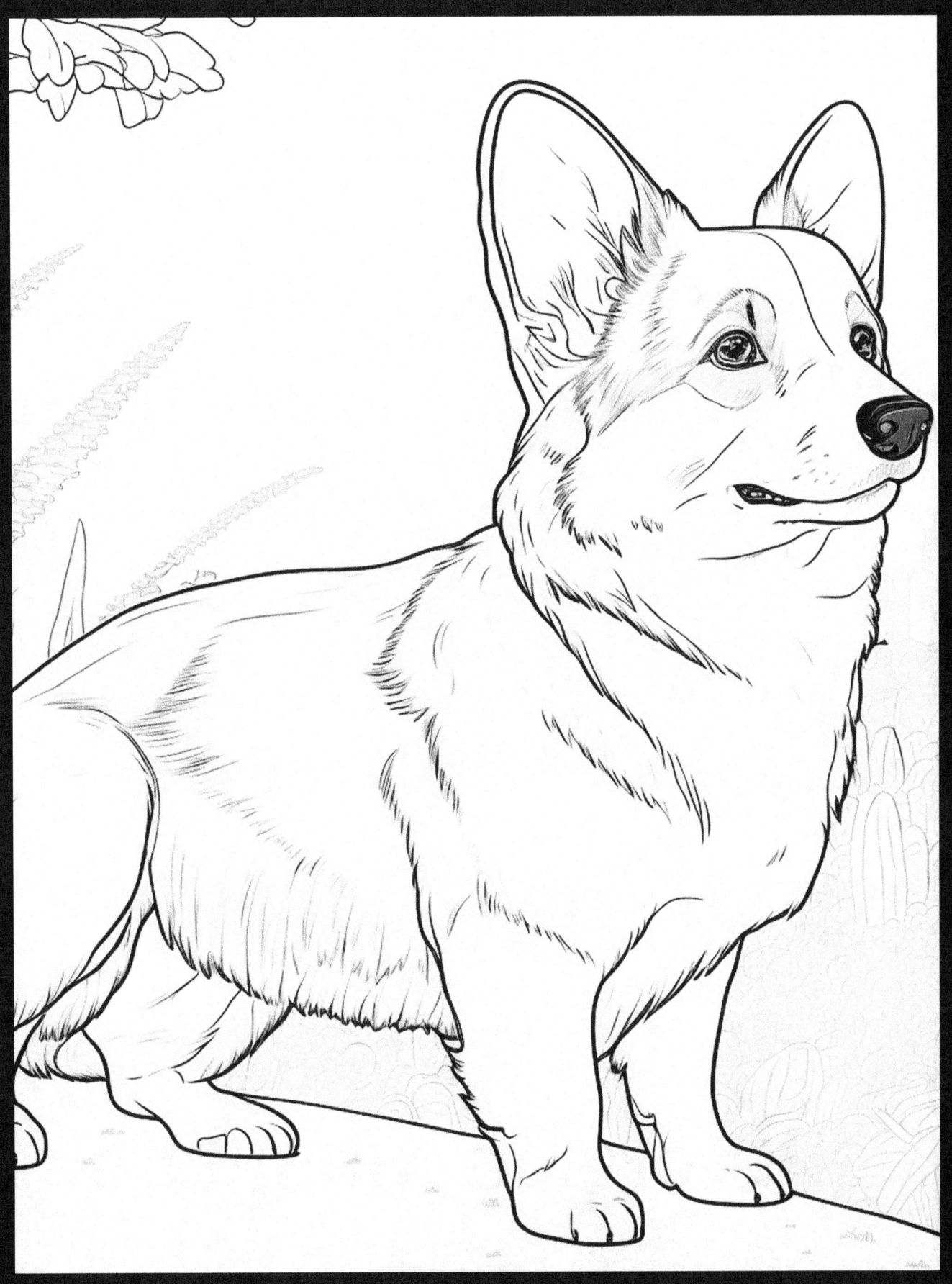

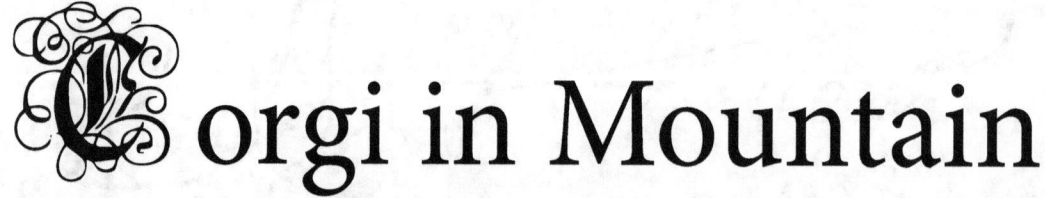

Corgi in Mountain

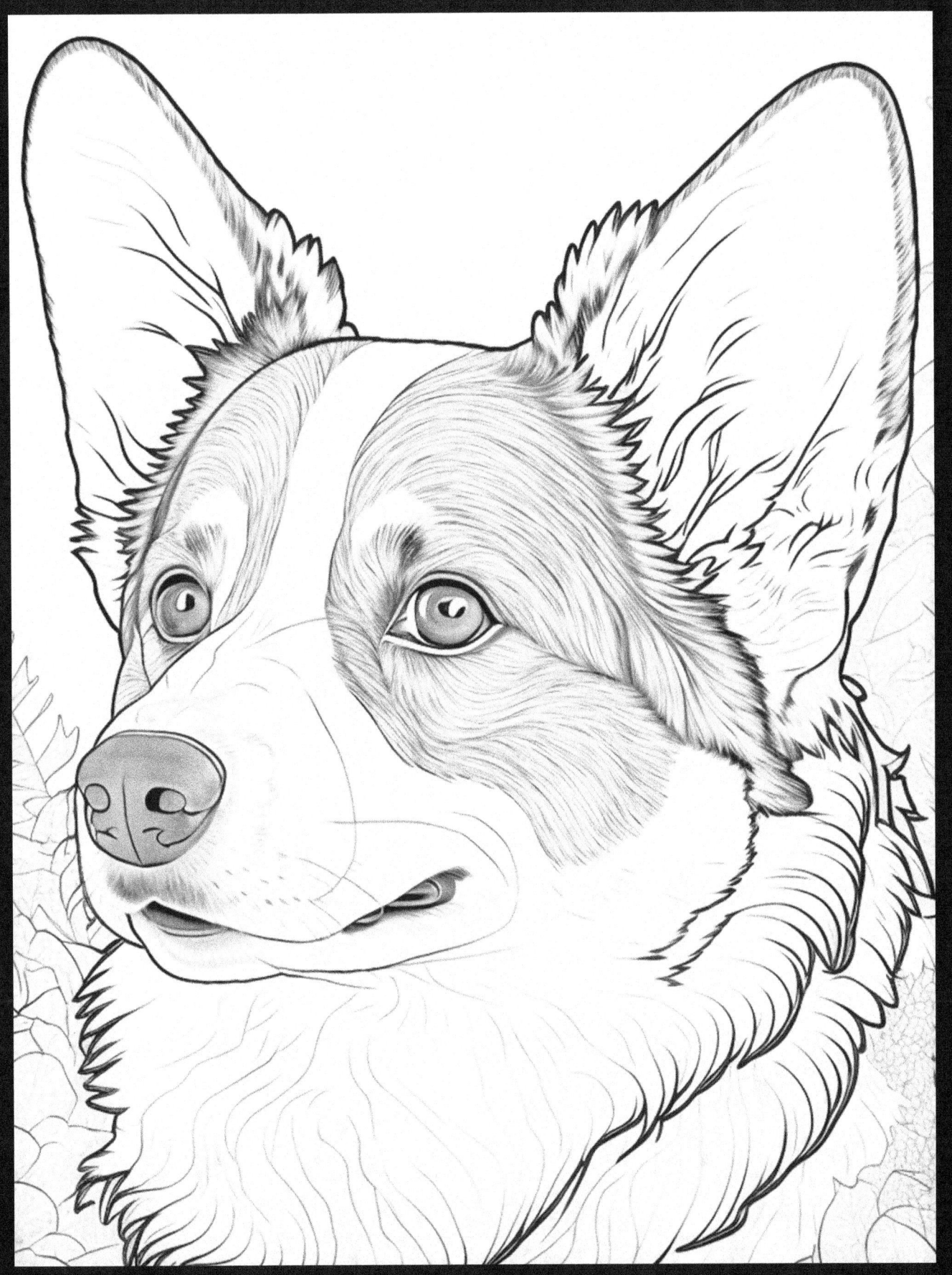

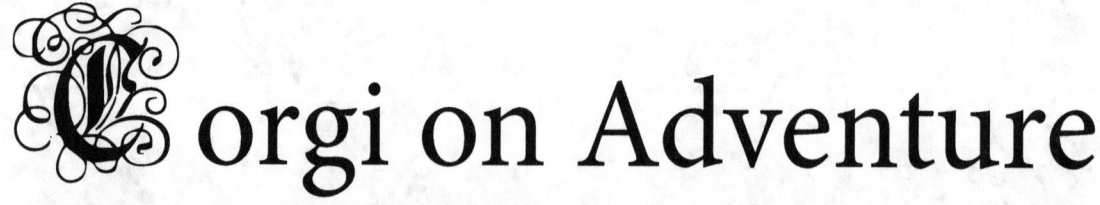

Corgi on Adventure

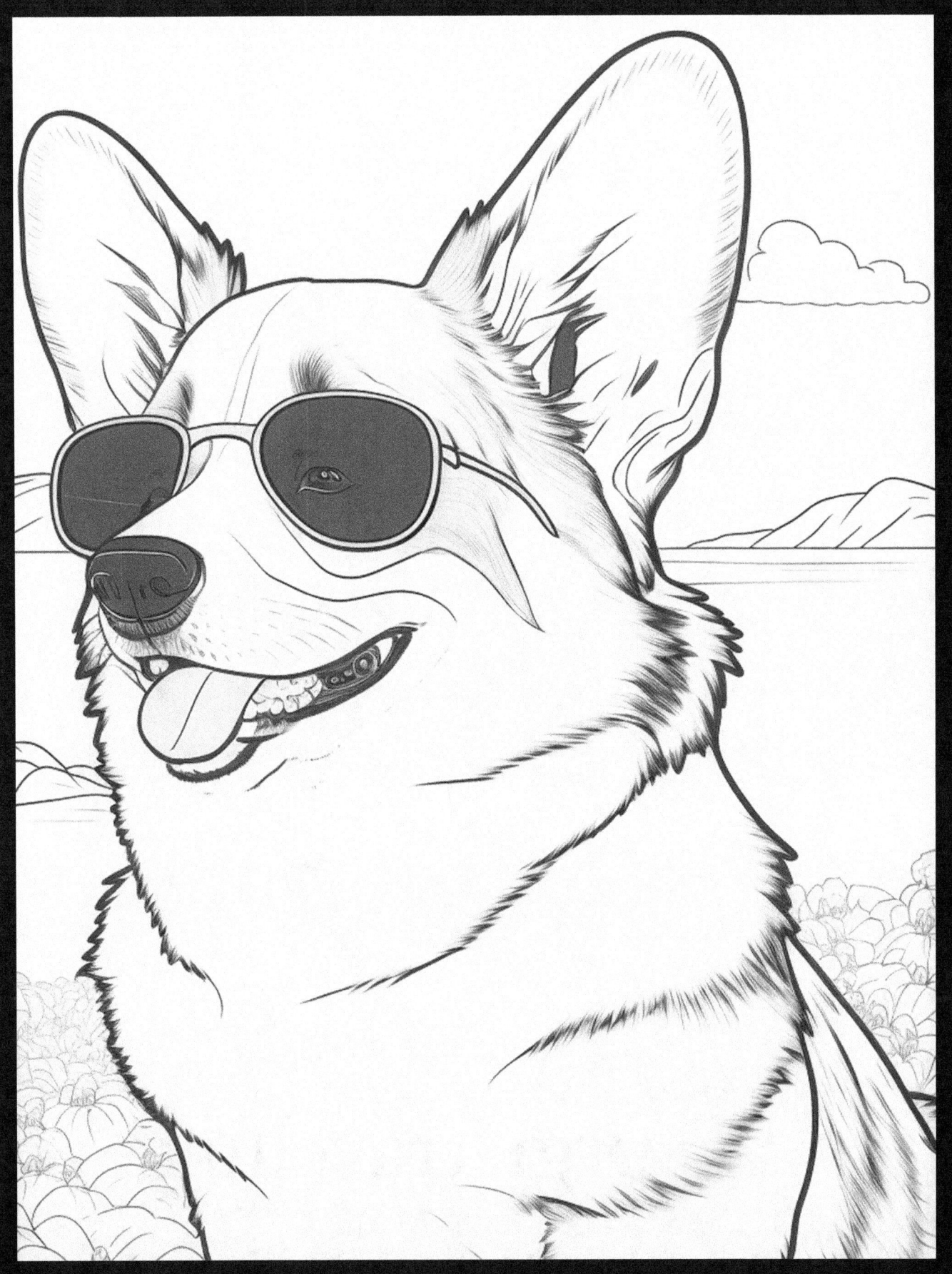

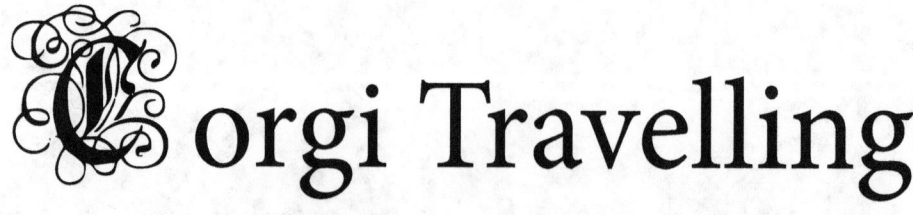

Corgi Travelling

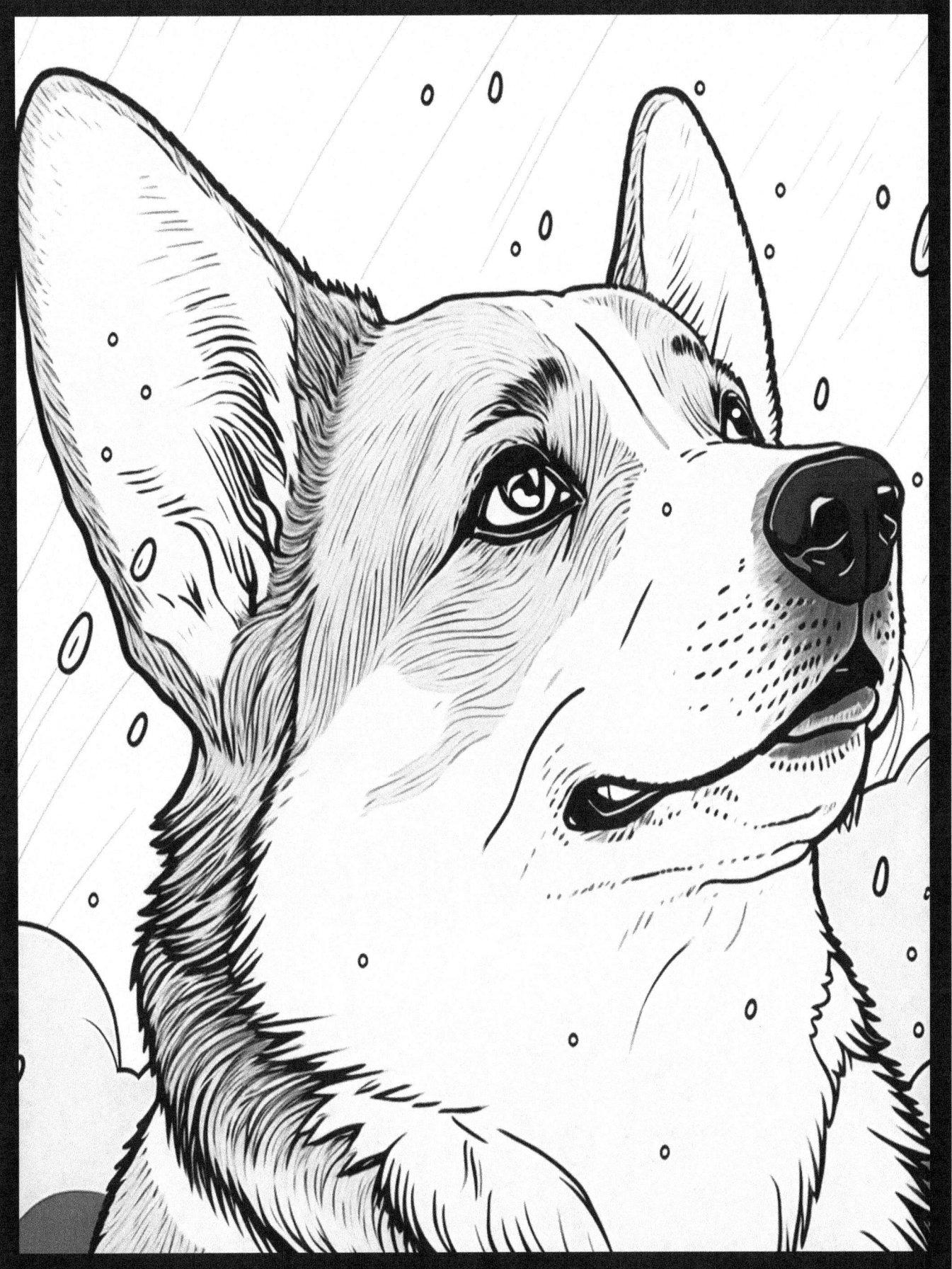

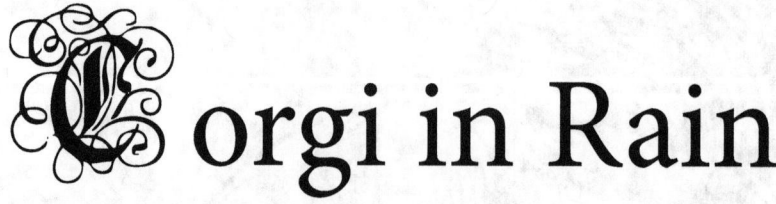

Corgi in Rain

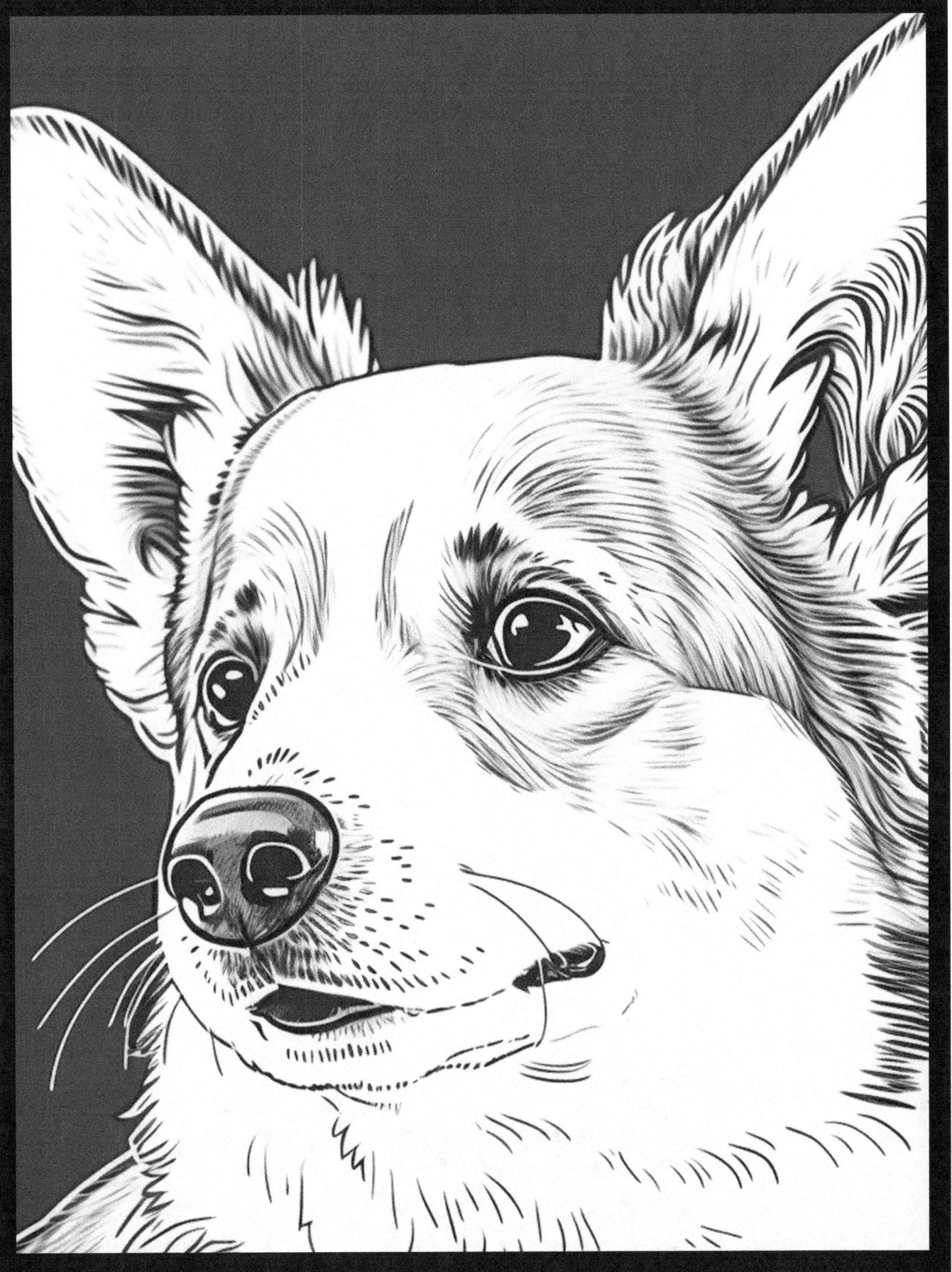

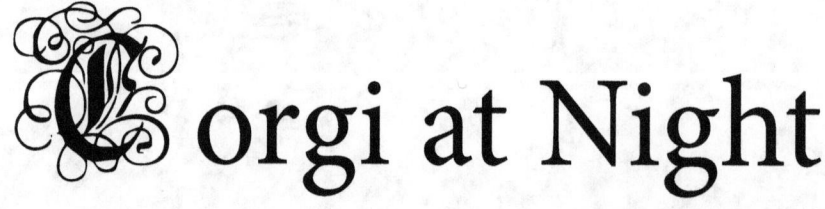

Corgi at Night

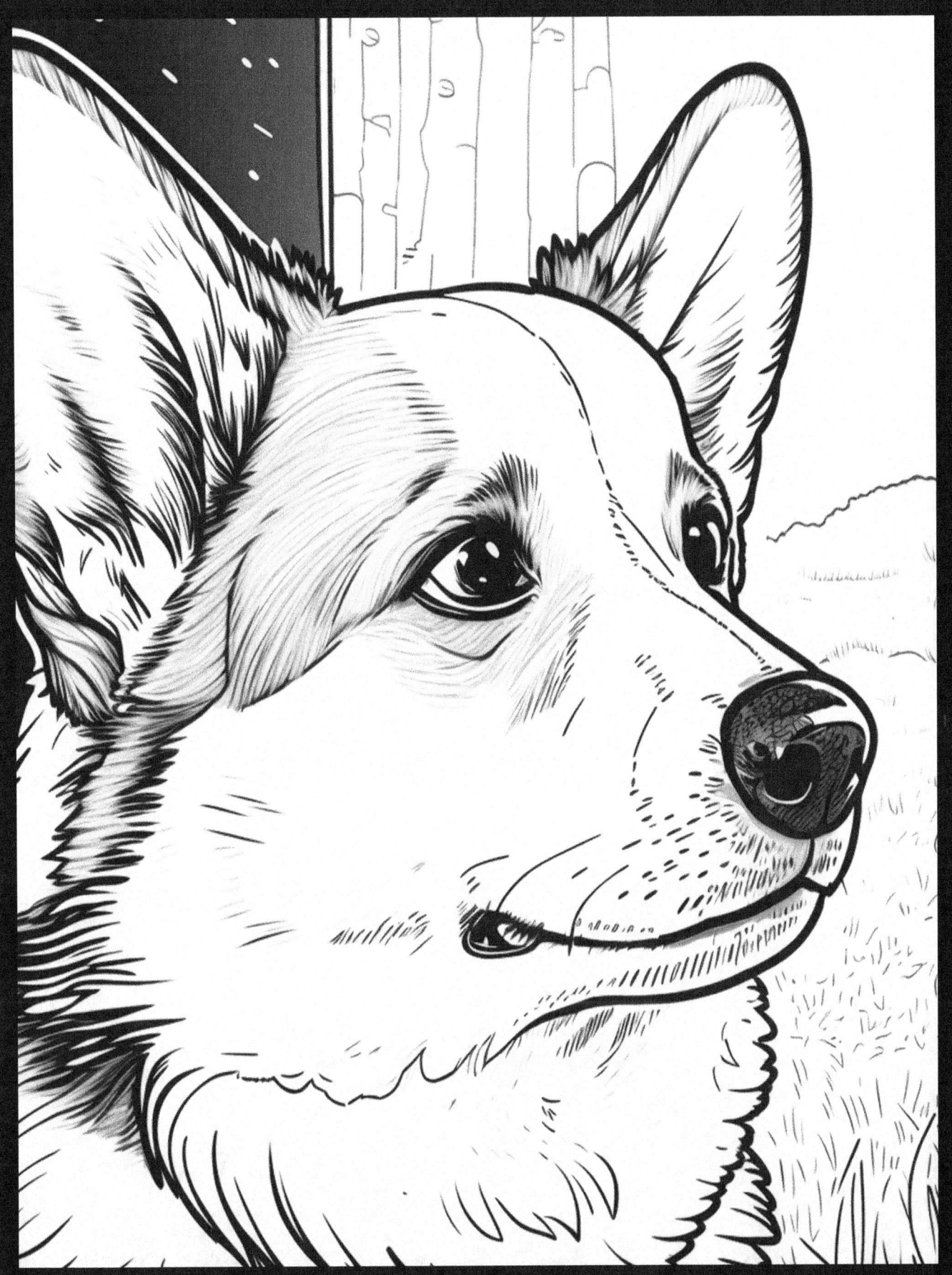

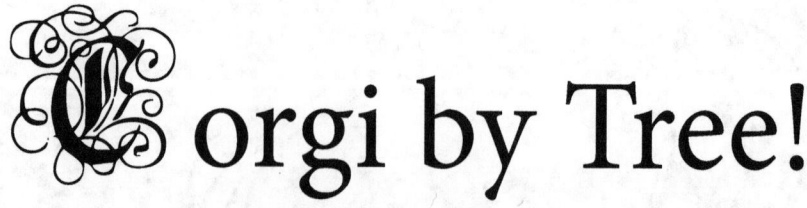
Corgi by Tree!

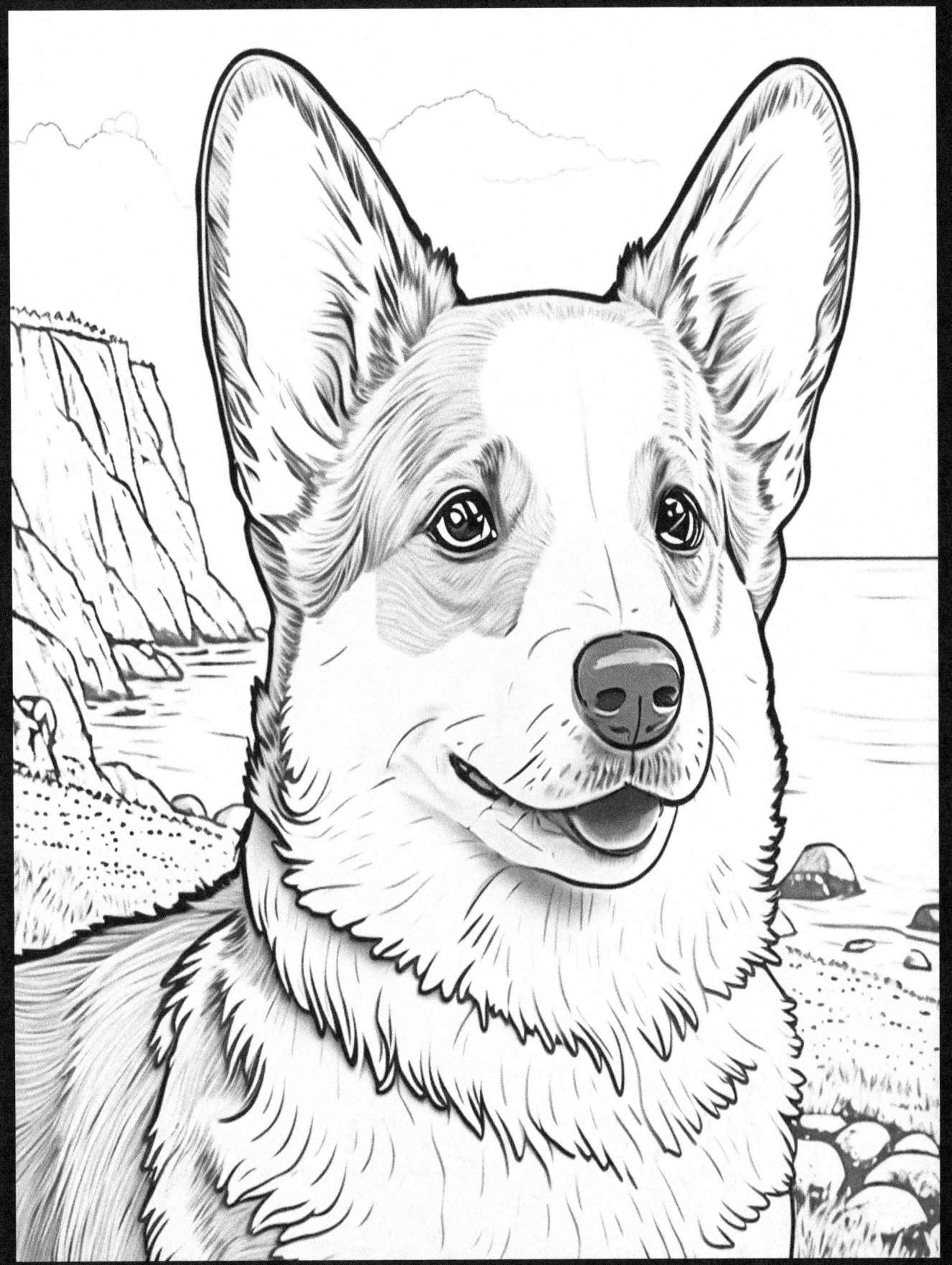

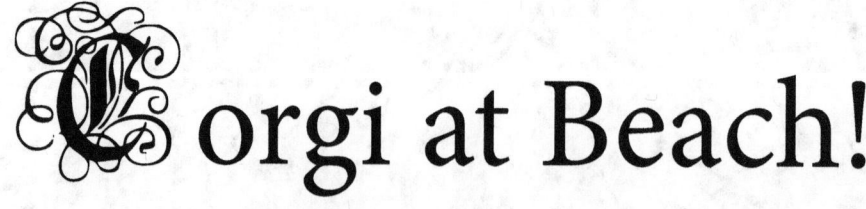

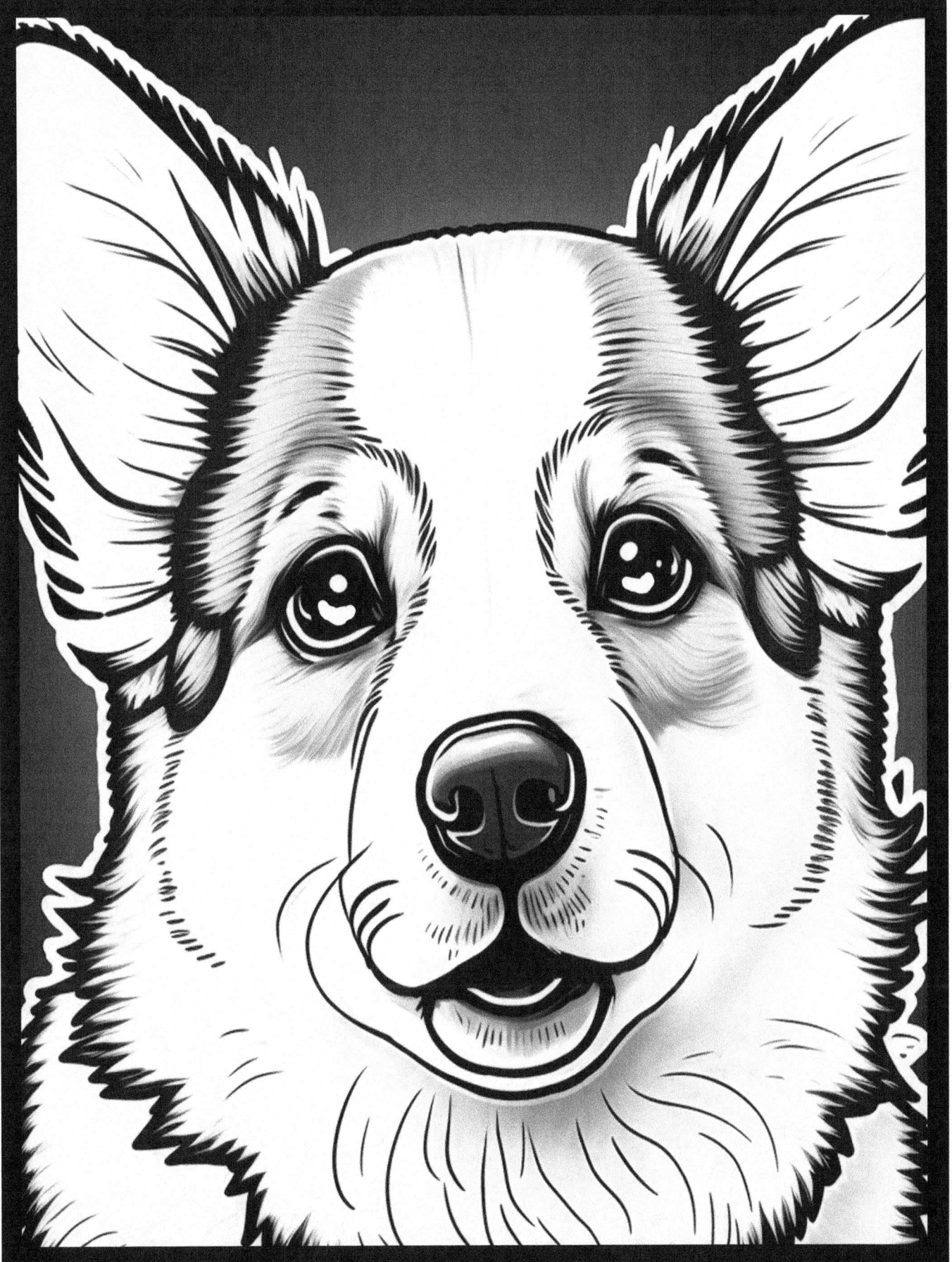

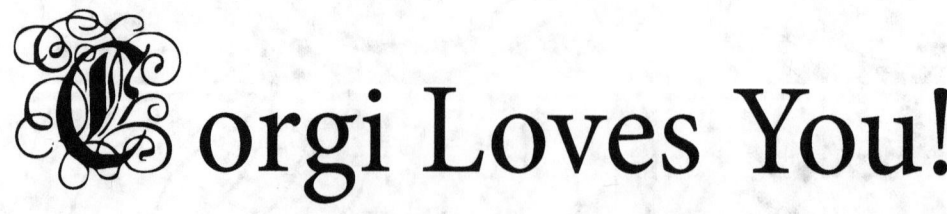

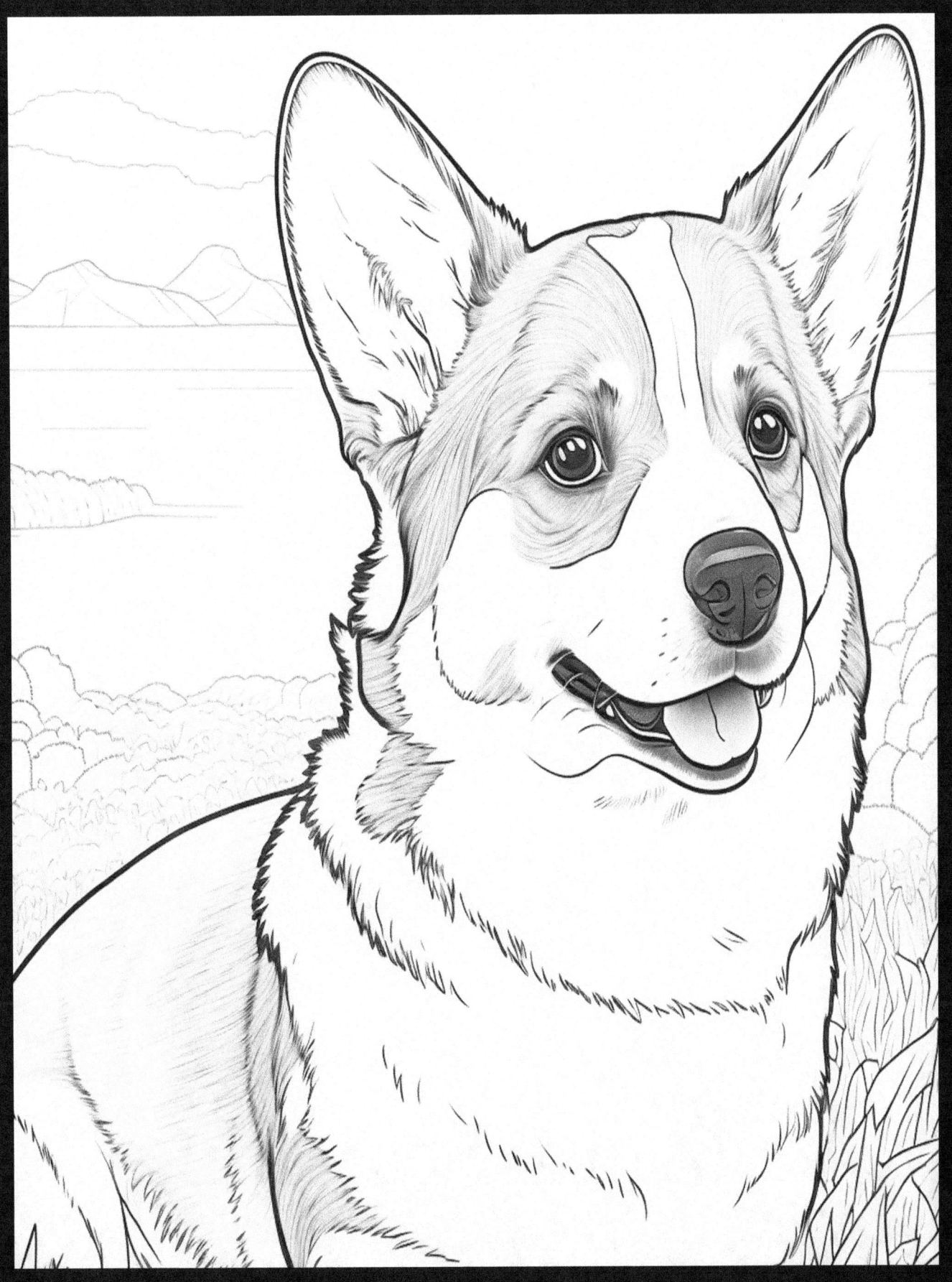

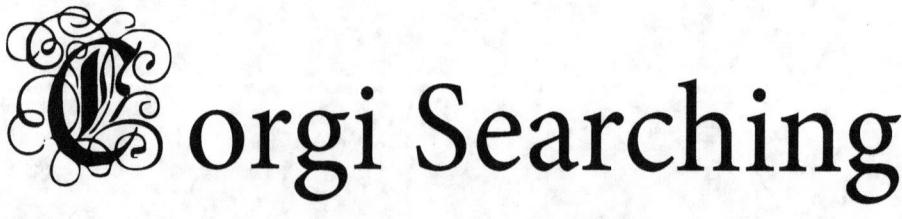

Corgi Searching

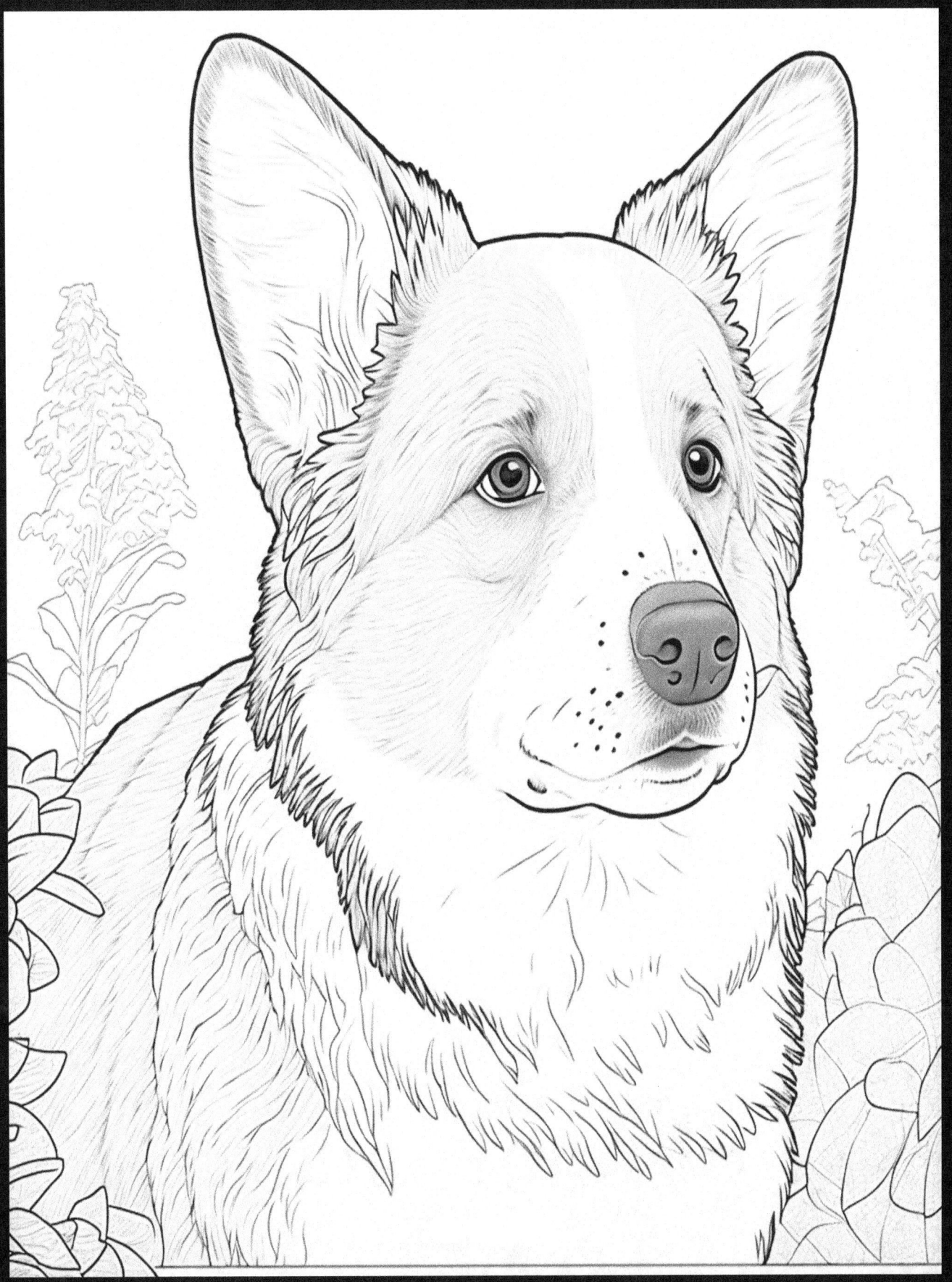

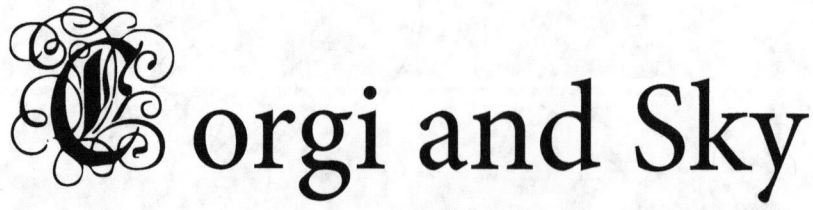

Corgi and Sky

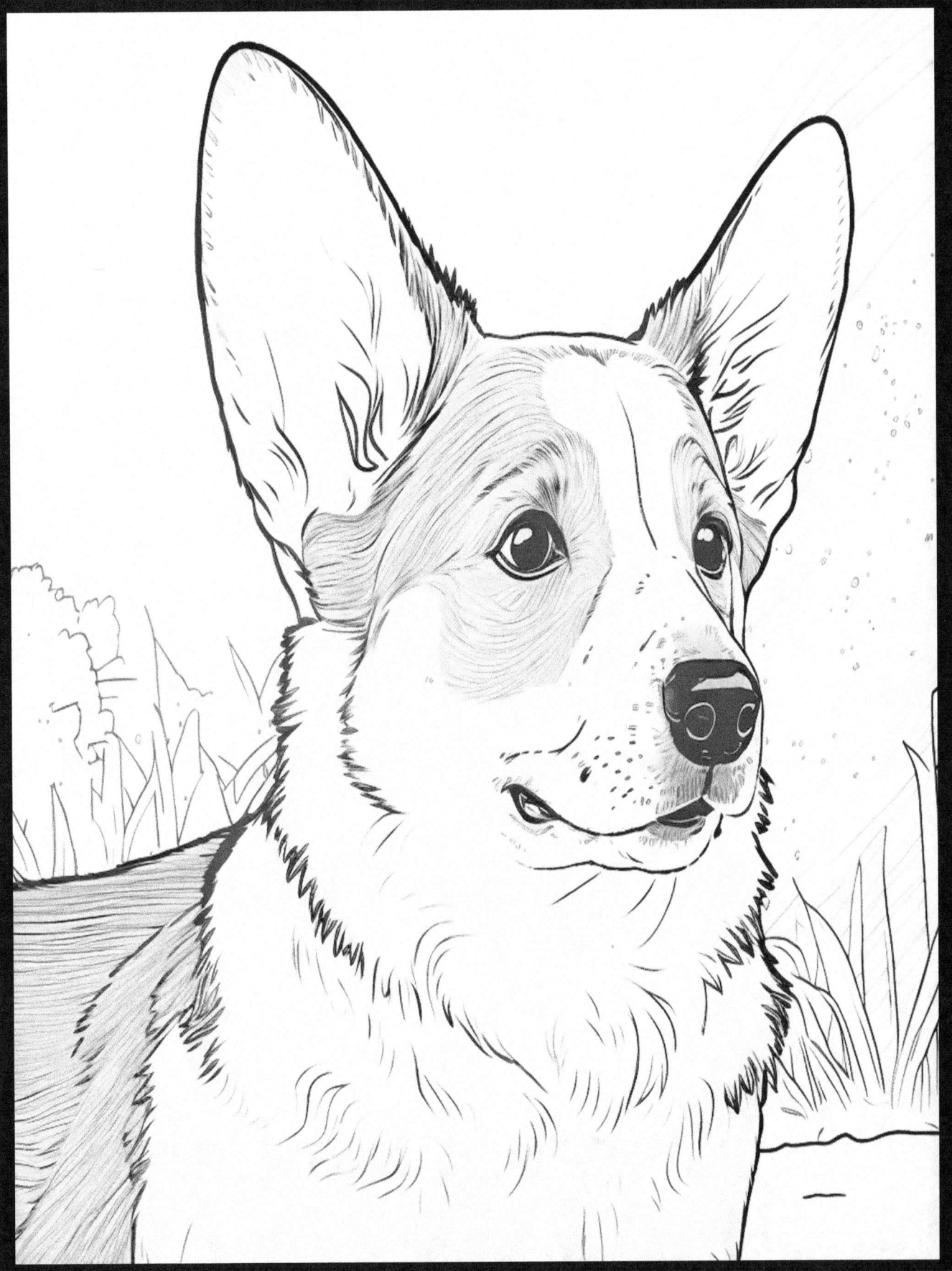

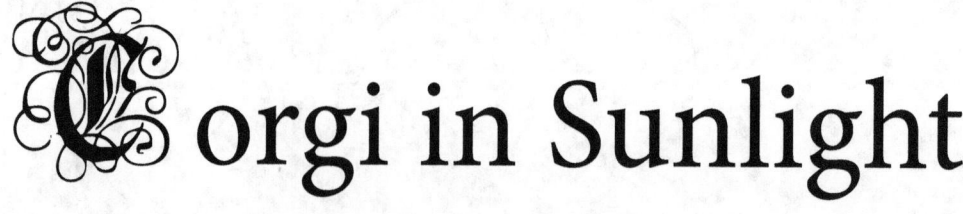

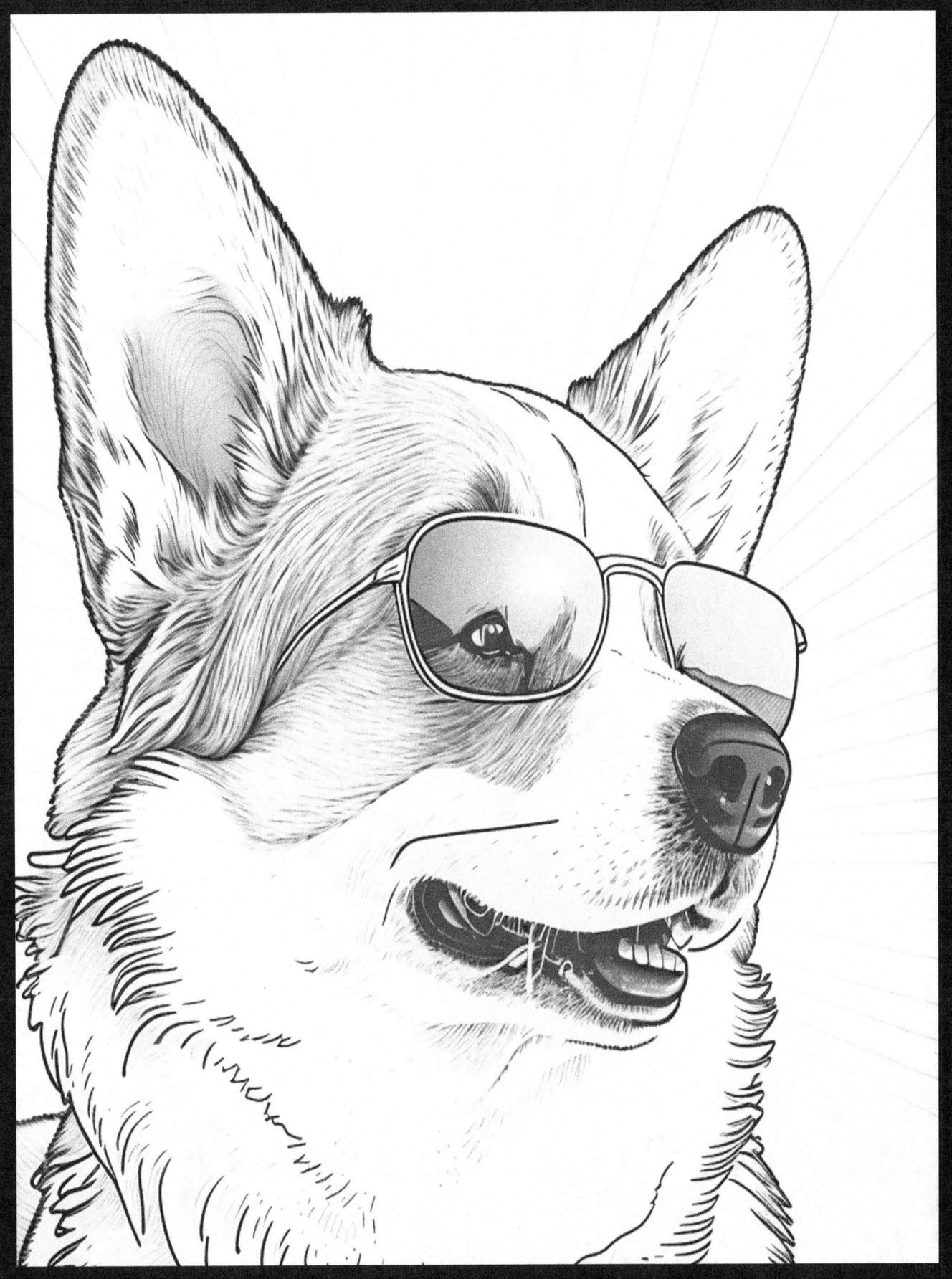

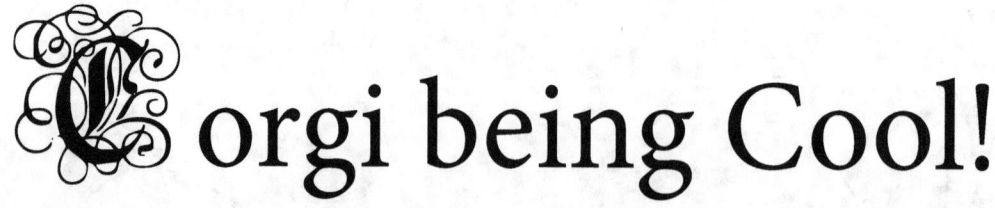

Corgi being Cool!

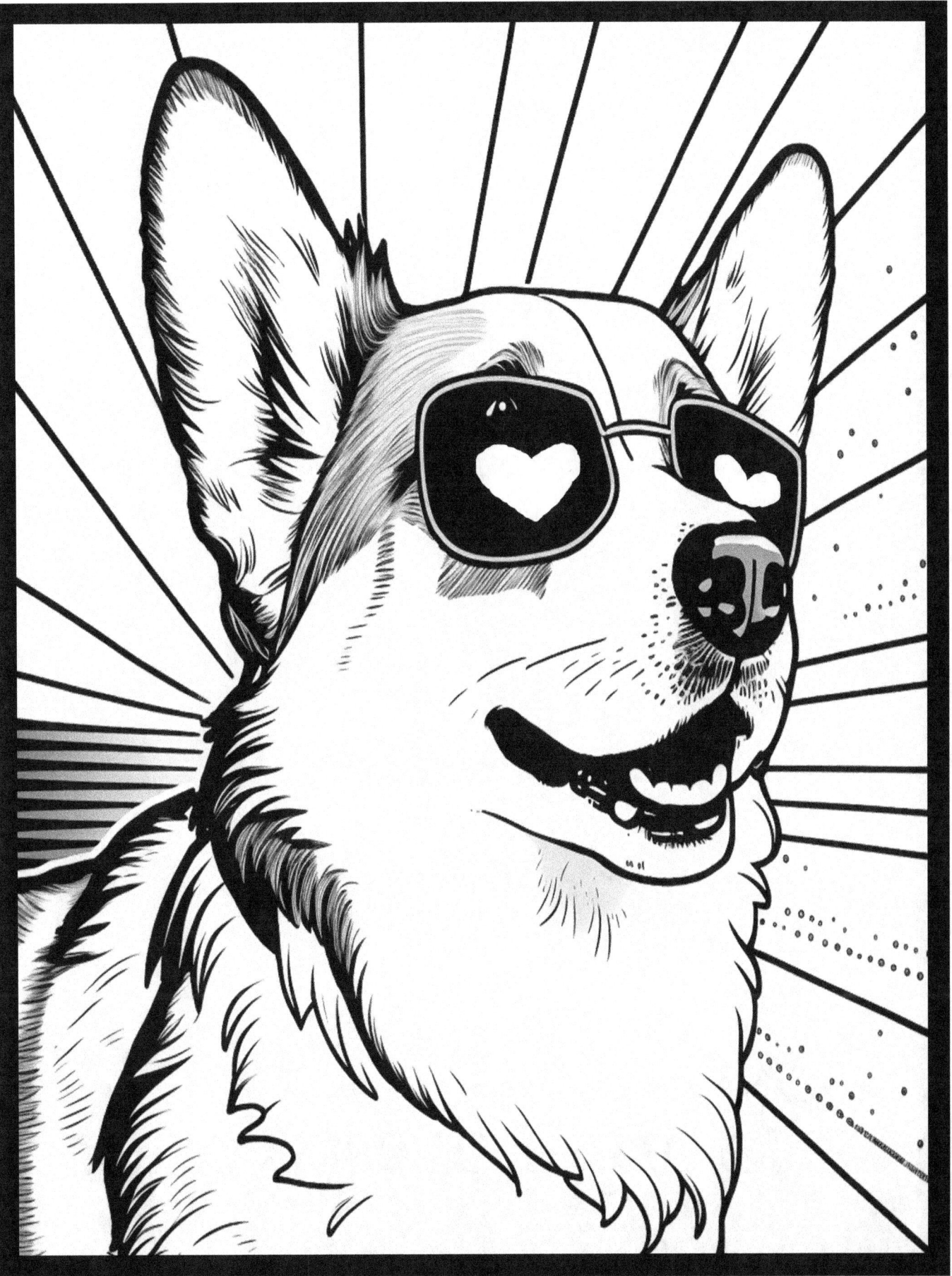

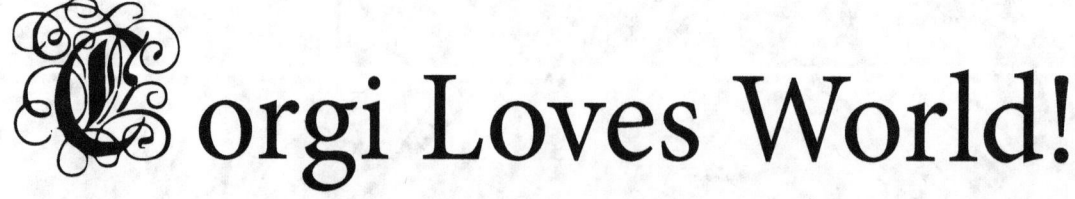

Corgi Loves World!

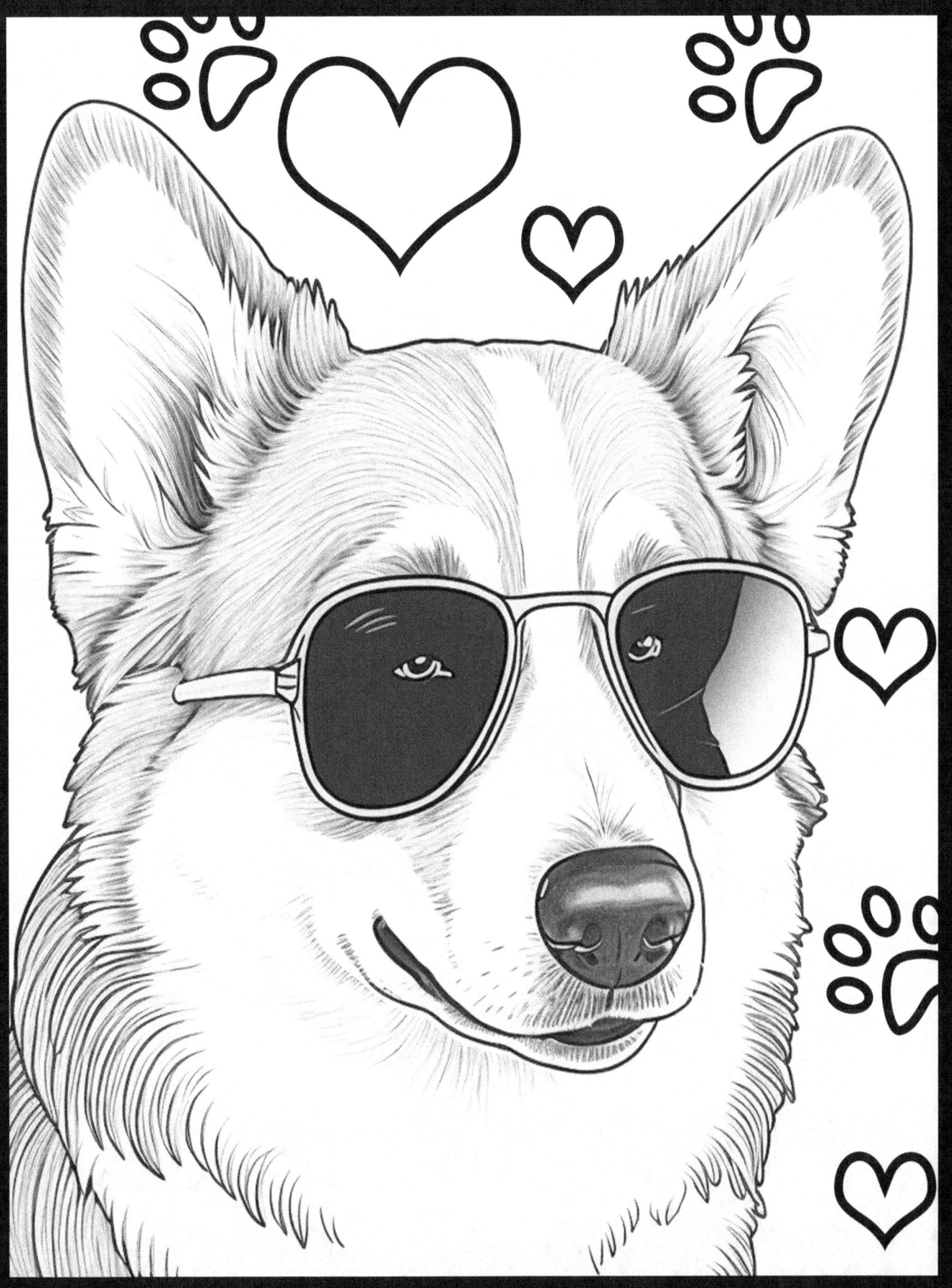

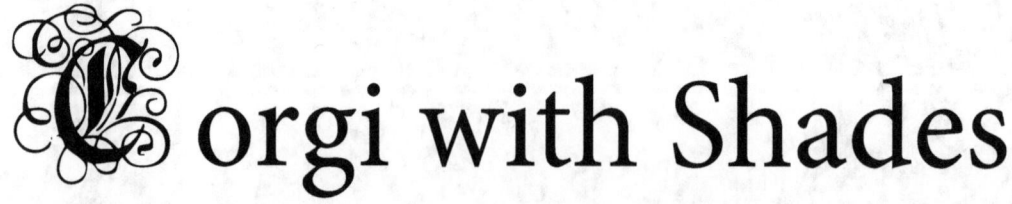
Corgi with Shades

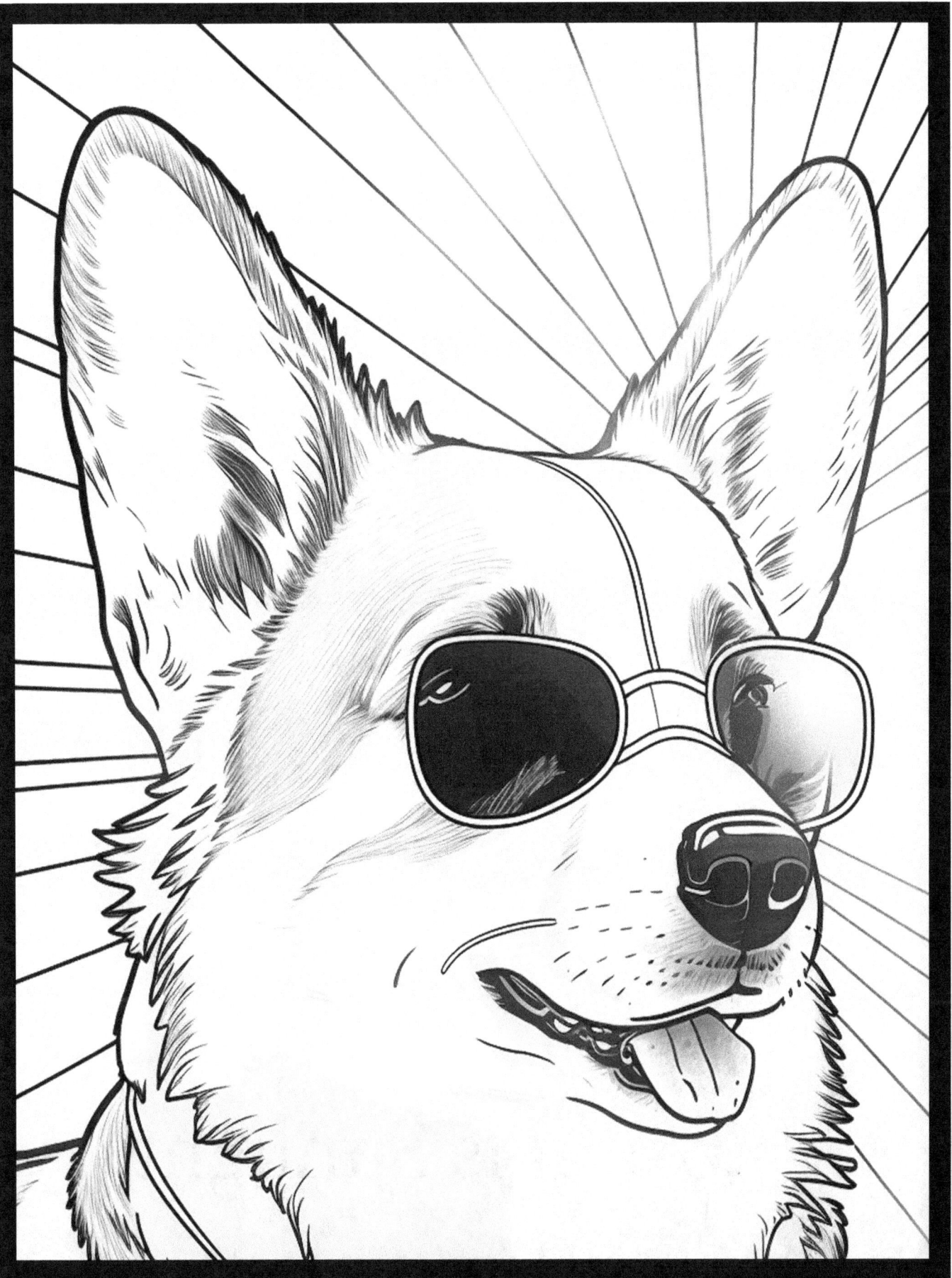

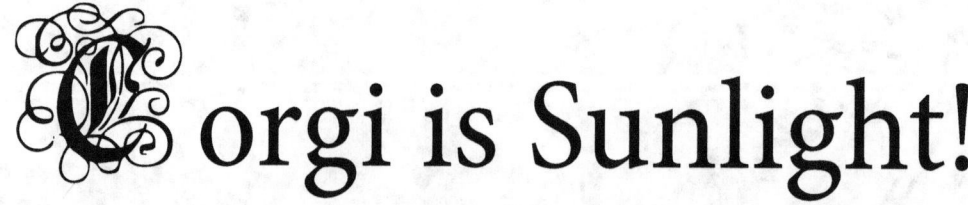

Corgi is Sunlight!

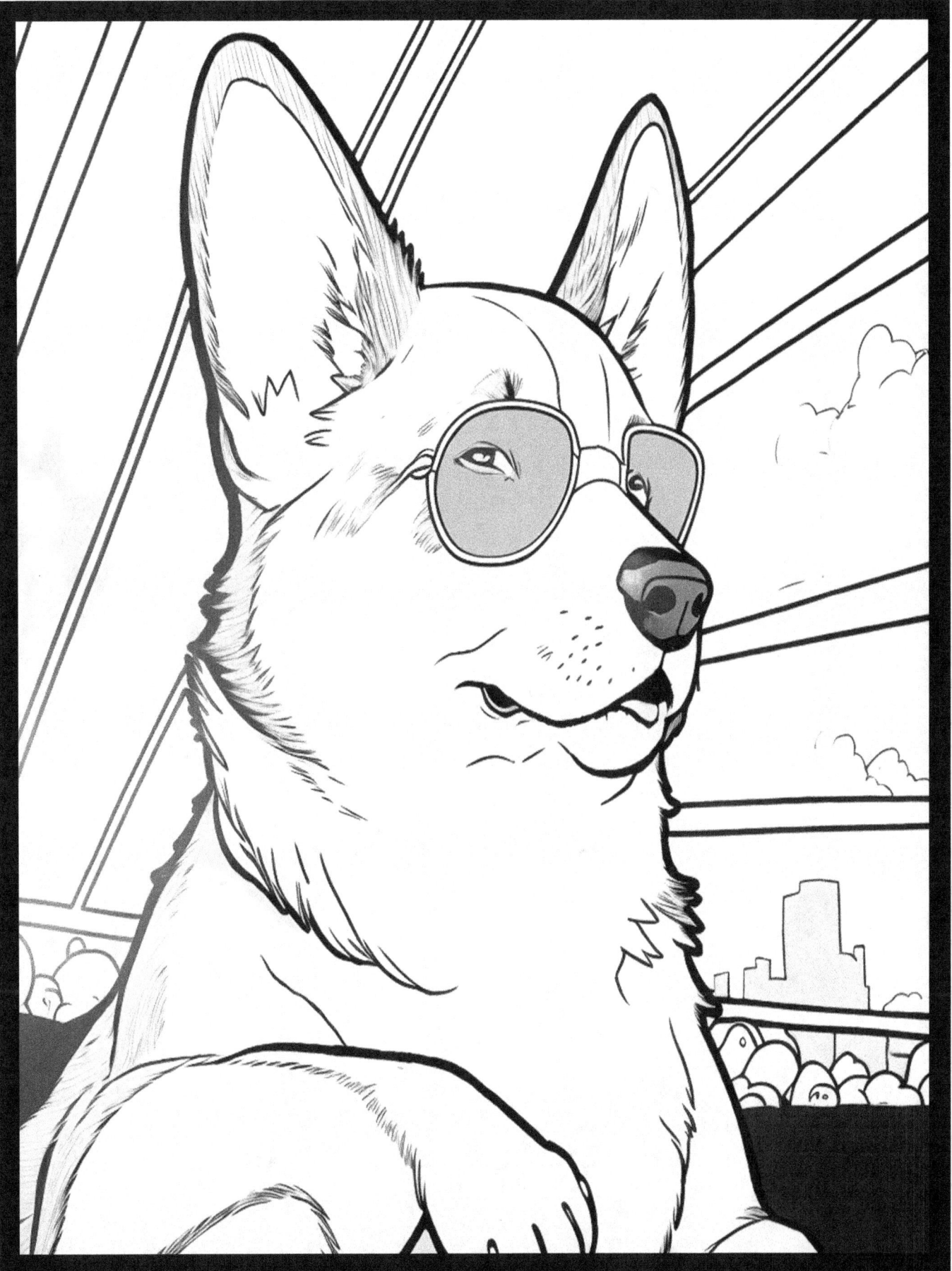

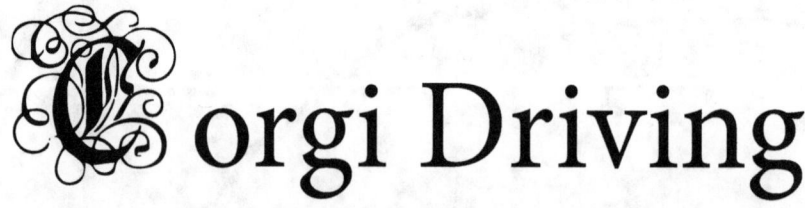
Corgi Driving

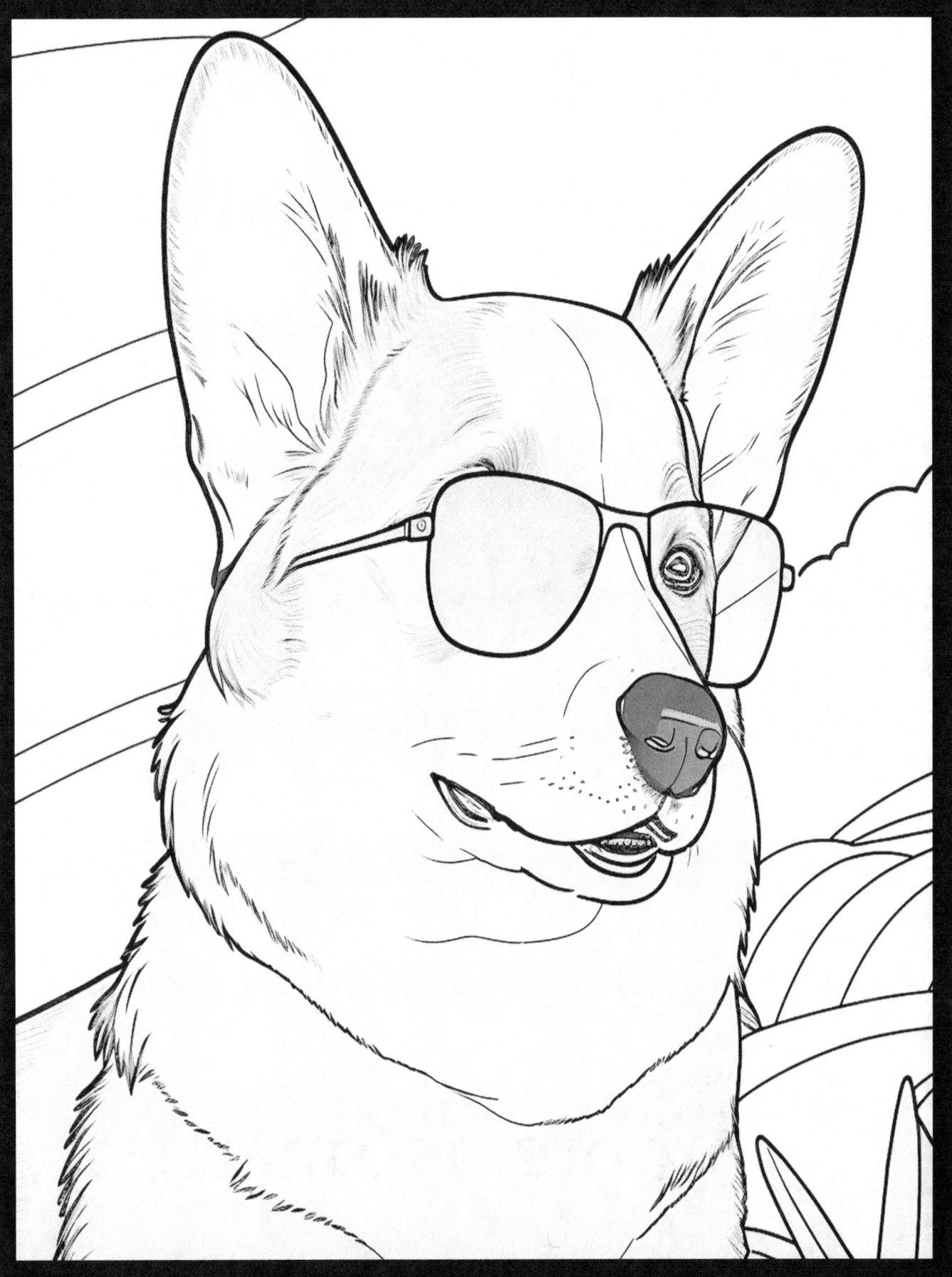

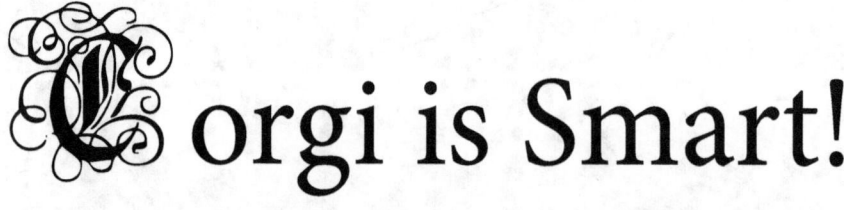

Corgi is Smart!

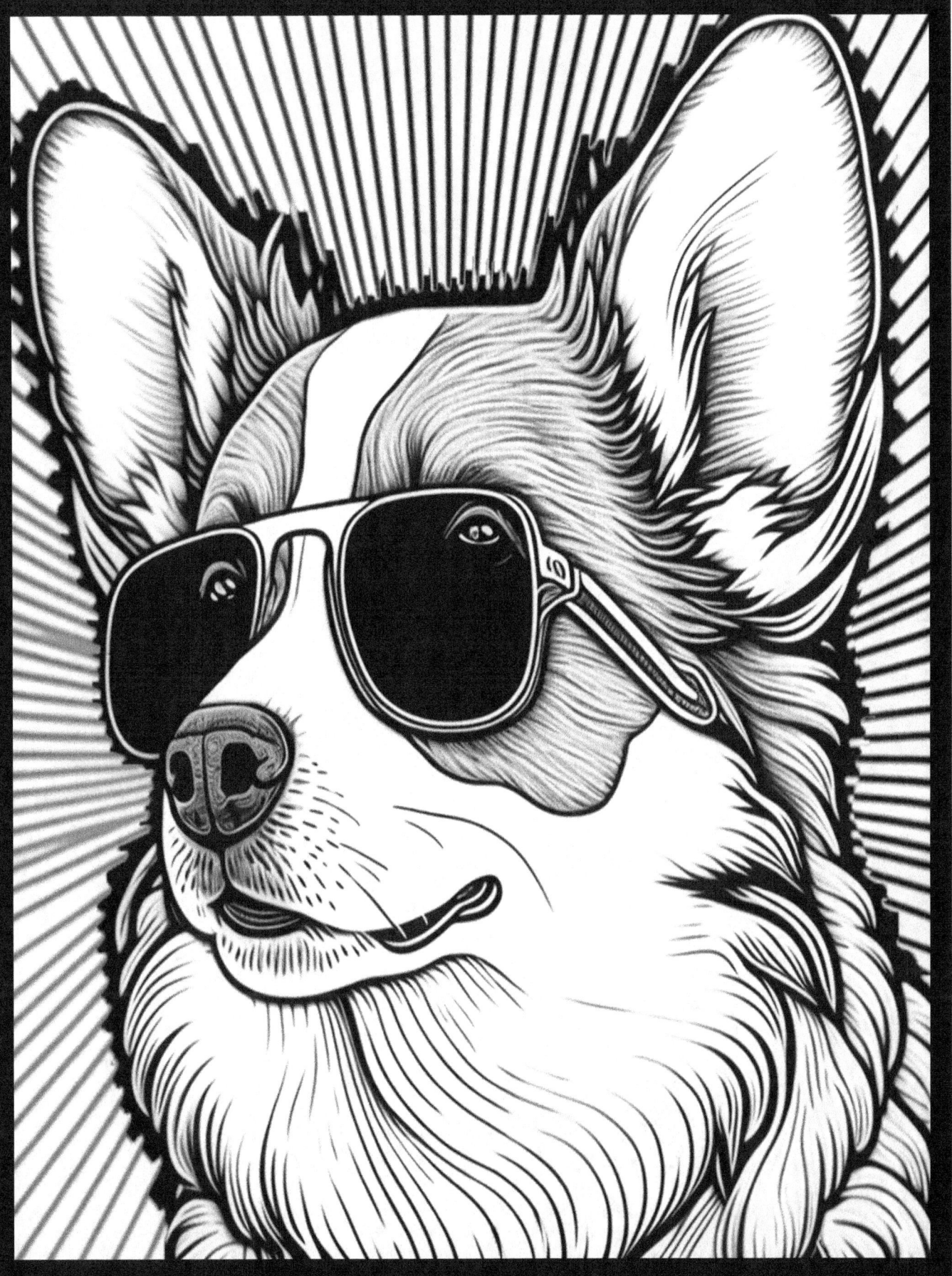

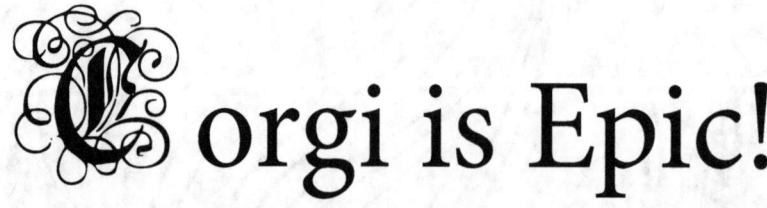

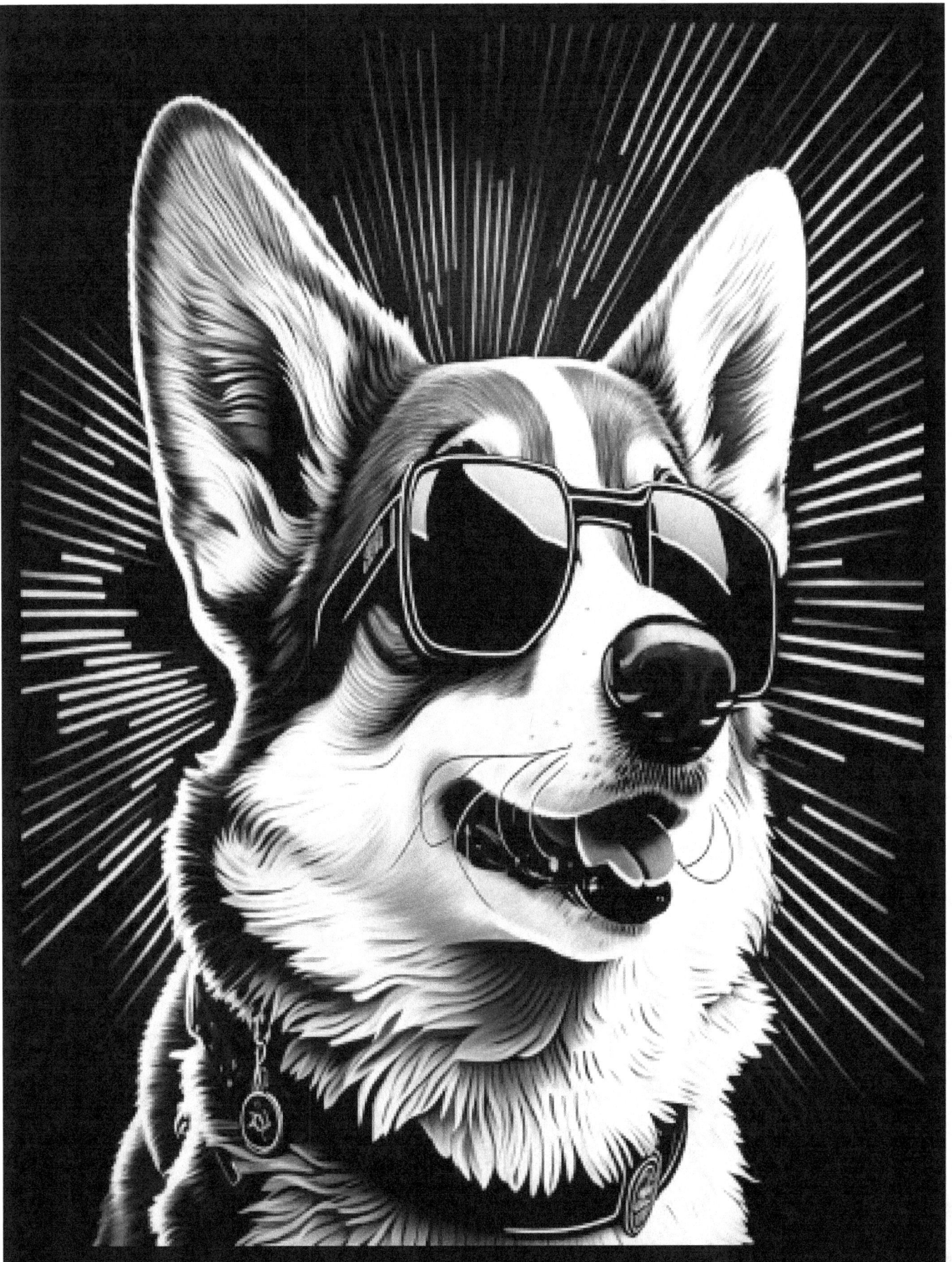

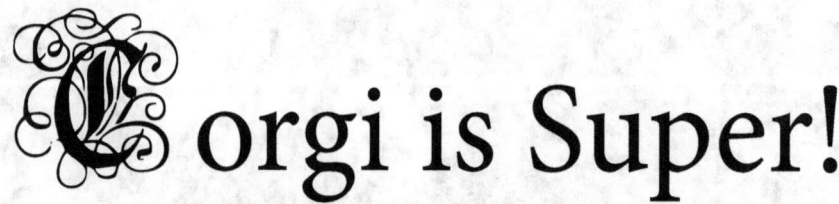
Corgi is Super!

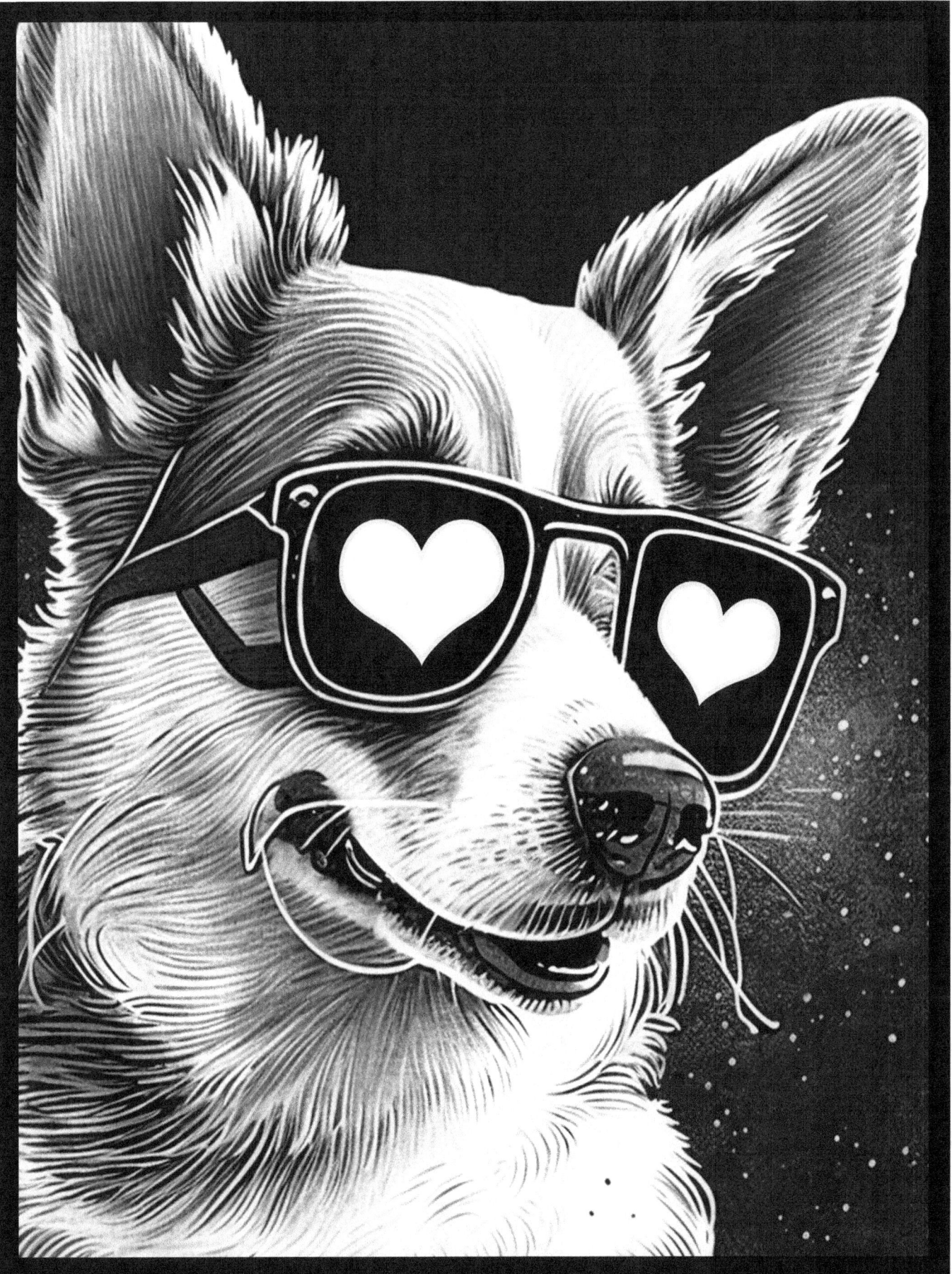

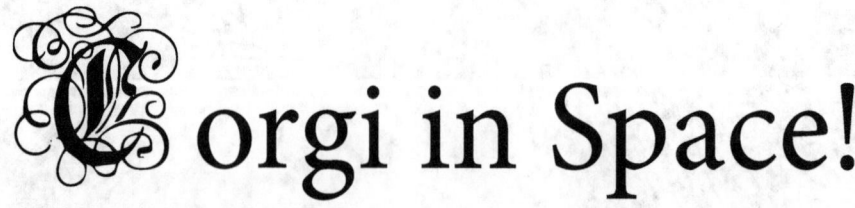

Corgi in Space!

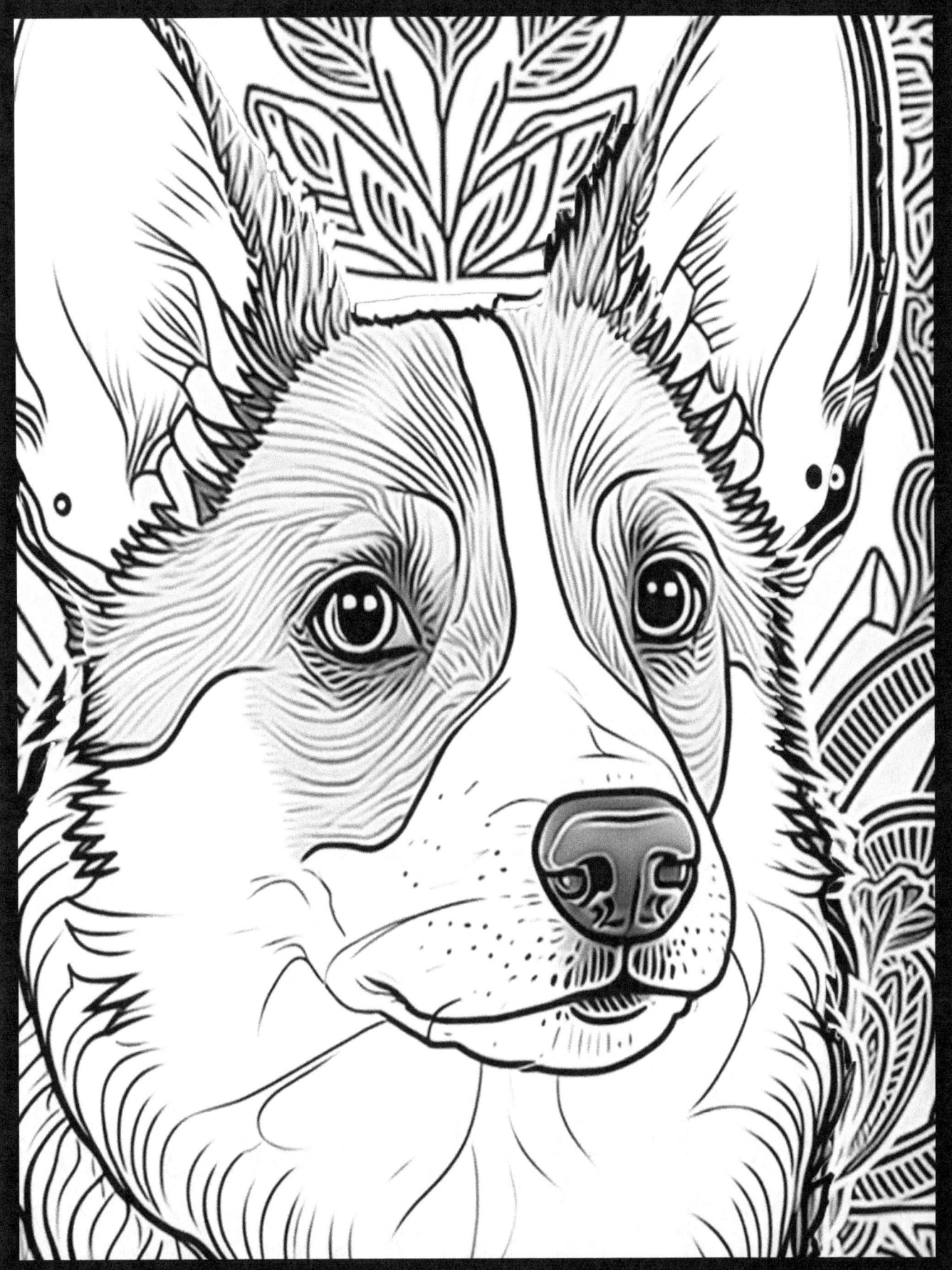

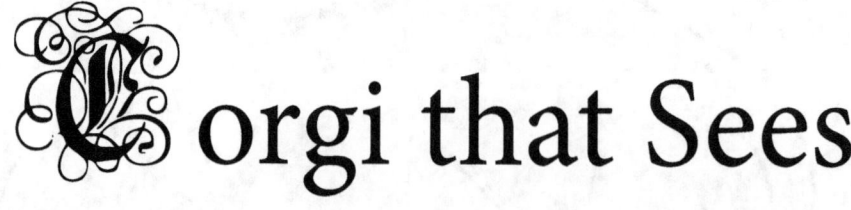
Corgi that Sees

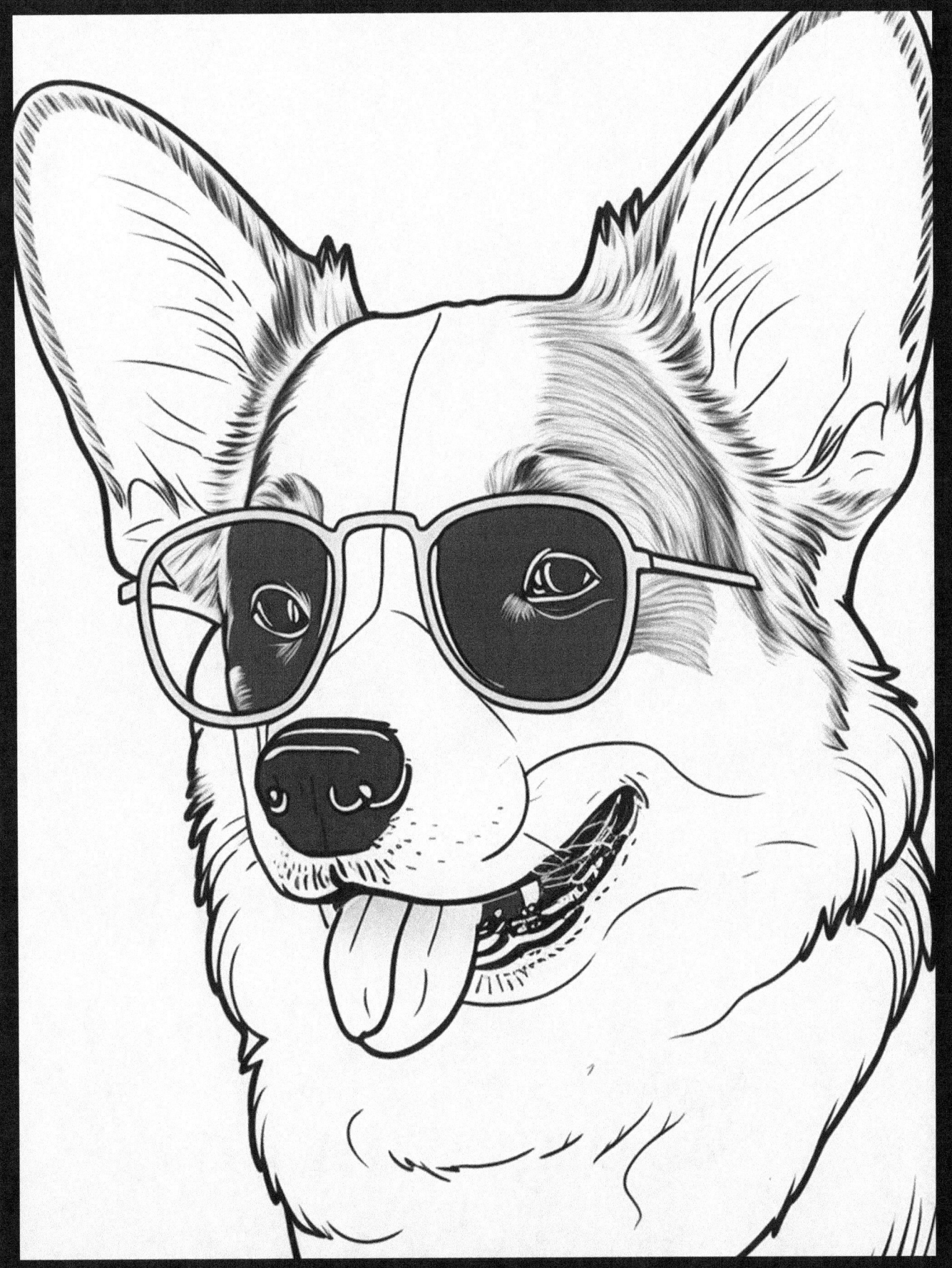

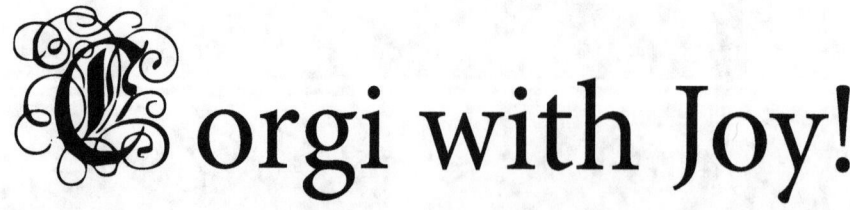
Corgi with Joy!

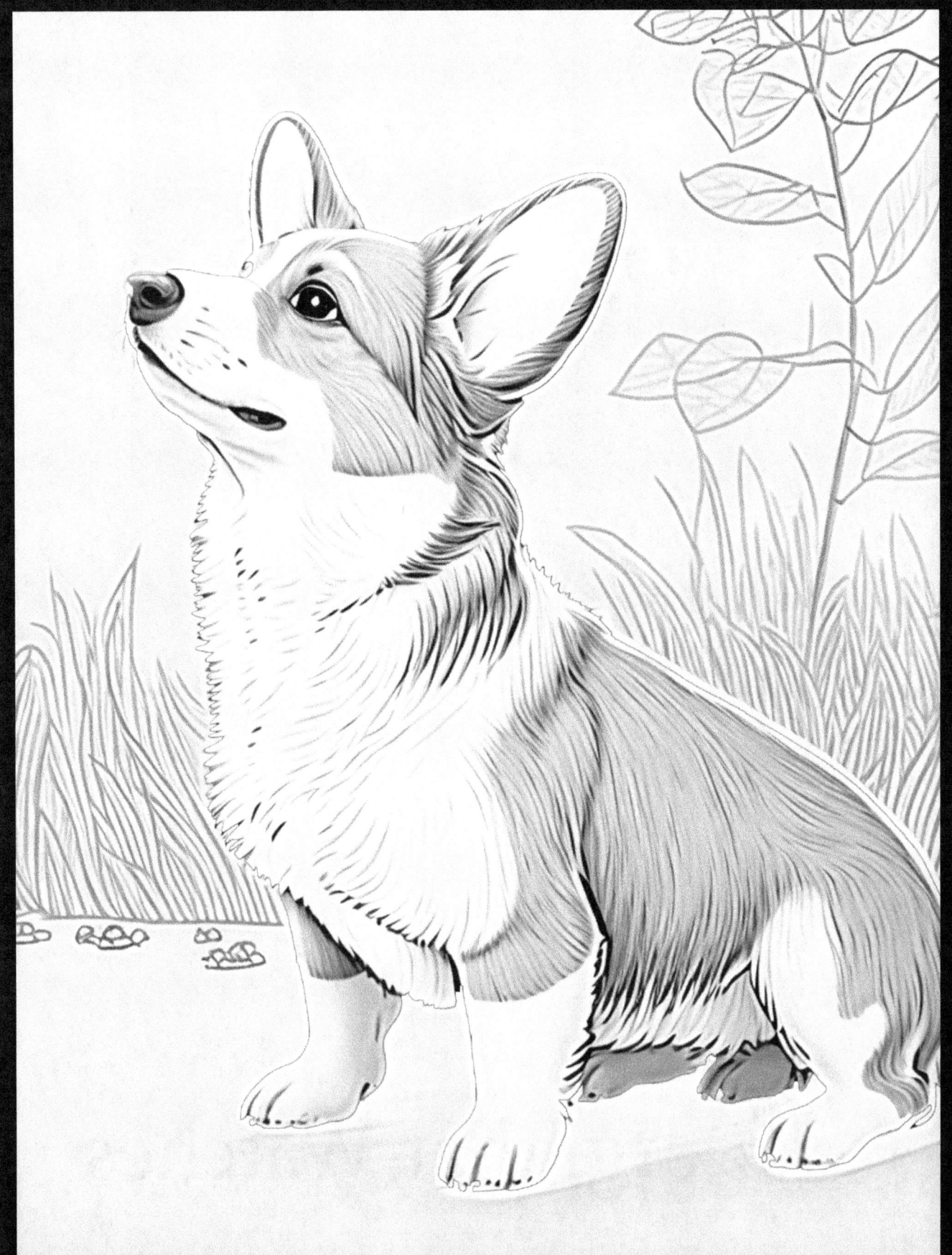

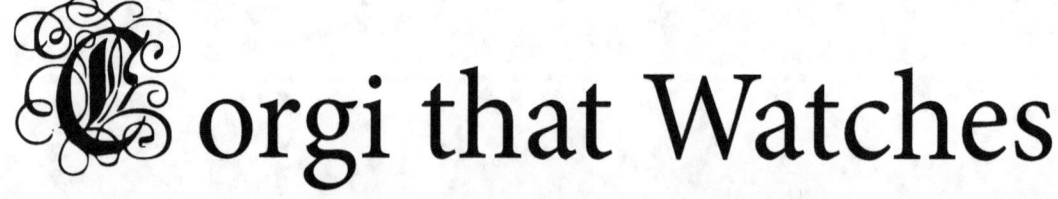

Corgi that Watches

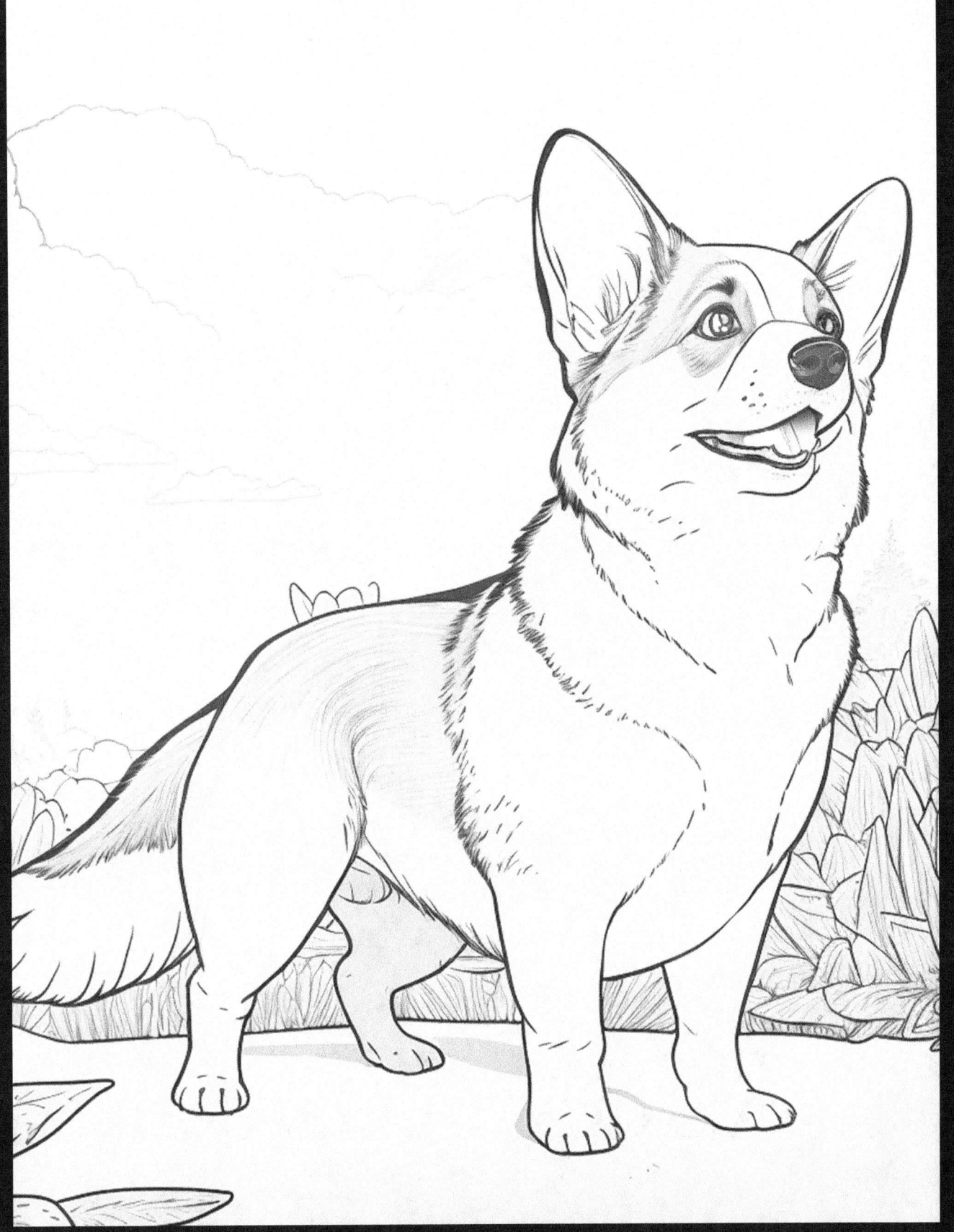

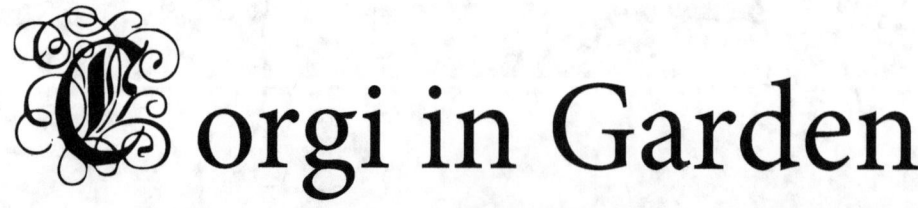

Corgi in Garden